Penguins

by Lucia Raatma

Content Advisers: Terrence E. Young Jr., M.Ed., M.L.S.,
Jefferson Parish (La.) Public Schools, and Janann Jenner, Ph.D.

Reading Adviser: Dr. Linda D. Labbo,
Department of Reading Education, College of Education,
The University of Georgia

COMPASS POINT BOOKS

Minneapolis, Minnesota

FIRST REPORTS

Compass Point Books
3722 West 50th Street, #115
Minneapolis, MN 55410

Visit Compass Point Books on the Internet at *www.compasspointbooks.com* or e-mail your request to *custserv@compasspointbooks.com*

Photographs ©: Robert McKemie/Daybreak Imagery, cover, 33, 34; John Gerlach/Visuals Unlimited, 4; Mary Ann McDonald, 5; Eda Rogers, 6; Joe McDonald, 7, 10, 13, 23; James Martin, 8, 18, 27; Daniel J. Cox/naturalexposures.com, 9, 26; Beth Davidow/Visuals Unlimited, 11; Kjell B. Sandved/Visuals Unlimited, 12, 29; Fritz Polking/Visuals Unlimited, 14, 16–17, 24; Dave Watts/Tom Stack & Associates, 15; Unicorn Stock Photos/Dick Keen, 19 (top); Frank Awbrey/Visuals Unlimited, 19 (bottom); Jessie M. Harris, 20; Stephen Frink/Corbis, 21; Gerald and Buff Corsi/Visuals Unlimited, 22, 32, 35, 36; Phyllis Greenberg/Colephoto, 30; Robin Karpan/Visuals Unlimited, 31; Albert Copley/Visuals Unlimited, 37; Unicorn Stock Photos/Travis Evans, 38; Ronald Cantor, 39; Joe McDonald/Visuals Unlimited, 41 (left); Janine Pestel/Visuals Unlimited, 41 (right); Photo Network/Darrell Jones, 42–43; XNR Productions, Inc., 46.

Editors: E. Russell Primm, Emily J. Dolbear, and Melissa Stewart
Photo Researcher: Svetlana Zhurkina
Photo Selector: Linda S. Koutris
Designer: Bradfordesign, Inc.

Library of Congress Cataloging-in-Publication Data
Raatma, Lucia.
    Penguins / by Lucia Raatma.
        p. cm. — (First reports)
    Includes bibliographical references and index.
    ISBN 0-7565-0058-3 (hardcover : lib. bdg.)
    1. Penguins—Juvenile literature. [1. Penguins.] I. Title. II. Series.
    QL696.S473 R32 2001
    598.47—dc21   00-010915

Table of Contents

On the Move

▲ *Penguins look funny when they walk!*

Penguins are birds, but they cannot fly. They walk on their flat feet. Some stand straight when they walk. Others seem to waddle from side to side. Penguins often look very funny when they walk.

Penguins are great swimmers and divers. They are covered with feathers that are almost waterproof.

▲ Penguins move easily in the water.

Their long bodies glide quickly through the water with ease.

When penguins swim, they flap their wings. Their wings work like flippers. They are "flying" underwater like birds fly in the air. They use their feet to steer.

Penguins swim as fast as 25 miles (40 kilometers)

per hour. That's about six times faster than a person can swim!

Penguins cannot breathe underwater. They must swim to the water's surface to breathe. Some penguins leap in and out of the water as they swim. Each

▲ *Penguins swim by flapping their wings underwater.*

▲ *In the water, some penguins leap like porpoises.*

time they leap, they take a breath of air. This way of swimming is called **porpoising**. Porpoises and dolphins swim the same way.

Penguins can jump too. To get out of the water, they jump onto the ground. They land flat on their feet. They often land on a rock or other hard surface.

▲ Penguins are great jumpers.

▲ *Instead of walking, some penguins slide on the ice.*

It is hard for a penguin to walk long distances. Instead, it slides along on its stomach. It pushes off with its wings and feet. A penguin can slide very quickly across the ice. This way of moving is called **tobogganing**.

What Do Penguins Look Like?

▲ *Most penguins are black and white.*

Penguins are mostly black and white. Their backs are black. Their stomachs are white. Some people think penguins look like they are wearing black-and-white suits called tuxedos. Male and female penguins usually look very much alike.

Their thick coats of feathers help keep penguins warm. The feathers are short and wide and grow close together.

Most penguins shed their feathers each year. Then they grow new ones. The process of losing and growing feathers is called **molting**.

Penguins have short tails. Their small wings stick

▲ *When penguins molt, they look very fluffy.*

▲ *A penguin has a long body and short legs.*

out from each side of their bodies. Their legs are short. Their feet are webbed. Penguins stand very straight.

The largest penguins are about 3 1/2 feet (106 centimeters) tall. They weigh almost 80 pounds (36 kilograms). That's about the same weight as a medium-sized dog.

Where Do Penguins Live?

▲ *Some penguins spend most of their lives in water.*

Some penguins spend three-fourths of their lives in the water. They may stay in the sea for months at a time.

All penguins live in the Southern Hemisphere. This part of the world lies south of the **equator**. Penguins live in Antarctica. They also live along the coasts of Africa, New Zealand, Australia, and South America.

▲ *These penguins live in Antarctica.*

▲ *This penguin lives on Macquarie Island, south of Australia.*

Living Together

▲ *Some penguin colonies contain thousands of birds.*

Penguins like company. Most penguins live together in groups called **colonies**. Thousands of them may

live in a single colony. Penguins often feed and swim in groups.

Penguins can "talk" to each other. They do not use words, of course. Instead, they use signals. They make special noises and movements. Penguins signal to each other as they work together to build nests.

▲ *Penguins communicate by making noises and motions.*

Penguins also call to one another. Each bird has a different call. A penguin's call helps its family members find the bird in a large crowd.

What Do Penguins Eat?

▲ *Penguins like to eat squid.*　　　　　　▼ *They also eat krill.*

Most penguins eat squid, fish, and **krill**. Krill are small sea animals that look like shrimp. Penguins have to eat lots of food to survive.

▲ *Penguins store a layer of fat in their bodies.*

Penguins catch their food as they swim. They swallow the food whole. These birds have powerful jaws to help them eat their food.

Many penguins can live for a long time without eating. They build up a thick layer of fat in their bodies. They can live off this store of fat until they find more food to eat.

▲ As penguins swim they find food to eat.

Penguins do not go into the water when they are molting. So, during this time, the birds must fast. To **fast** means "to stop eating." Penguins also fast when they take care of the eggs in their nests.

▲ *Penguins eat nothing while taking care of the eggs in their nests.*

Baby Penguins

▲ *Penguin parents take turns caring for the eggs in the nest.*

Most penguins build nests of pebbles and a few small plants. The mother penguin lays one or two eggs. The mother and father take turns sitting on

▲ After an emperor penguin egg hatches, the mother returns to take care of the chick.

the eggs to keep them warm. The parent taking care of the eggs does not eat while the other parent is away.

One type of penguin is called the emperor penguin. This kind of penguin takes care of its eggs in an unusual way. The emperor penguin lays just one egg. Then the mother goes away to look for food. The father penguin takes care of the egg by himself for many months.

Emperor penguins don't build nests. The father holds the egg on top of his foot. He tucks it under a fold of his belly to keep it warm.

When the egg hatches, the mother penguin comes back. She takes care of the young penguin. The father is then free to eat and rest.

Some types of birds are a danger to penguins. These birds hunt and eat penguin eggs and **chicks**. To keep their babies safe, the mother and father penguins guard their young for a long time.

▲ *Other birds sometimes eat penguin eggs and chicks.*

Usually, one parent watches the nest while the other hunts for food.

Baby penguins are born with a fluffy coat of

▲ *Baby penguins are fluffier than their parents.*

feathers. The feathers may be white, gray, black, or brown. But these feathers are not yet waterproof. Chicks must stay out of the water until they have their adult feathers. It usually takes one year for the adult feathers to grow.

During that first year, baby penguins prepare to be adults. They eat a lot of food. This gives them strength for their first molting.

Types of Penguins

▲ *Emperor penguins*

There are seventeen different kinds of penguins. The emperor penguin is the largest and the most common. It grows to be 4 feet (1.2 meters) tall. The emperor penguin has a black head, chin, and throat. It has yellow ear patches on the sides of its head.

The king penguin is a little smaller than the emperor penguin. It is usually about 3 1/2 feet (1 meter) tall. This penguin has bright orange ear patches. It usually has orange patches on its chest too.

The yellow-eyed penguin is about 30 inches (76 centimeters) tall. It has yellow feathers on the sides of its head. It also has bright yellow eyes.

▲ A king penguin

▲ *Yellow-eyed penguins*

▲ *A gentoo penguin*

The gentoo penguin has a white patch over each eye. The patches are usually shaped like triangles. This penguin is about 24 to 30 inches (60 to 76 centimeters) tall.

▲ *An Adélie penguin*

The Adélie penguin is 18 to 24 inches (45 to 60 centimeters) tall. It has white rings around its eyes.

A *chinstrap penguin*

The chinstrap penguin has a black stripe under its chin. The stripe looks like the chin strap on a hat—which is how this penguin got its name. The chinstrap penguin is about 18 to 24 inches (45 to 60 centimeters) tall.

The smallest penguin is the little blue penguin. It is also called the fairy penguin. This bird has blue-gray eyes. It lives in Australia and New Zealand. It is only about 12 inches (30 centimeters) tall.

Other kinds of penguins include the macaroni, the rockhopper, and the royal. There are also six kinds of crested penguins, named for the tufts of yellow

▲ A macaroni penguin

feathers on the sides of their heads. These feathers are called **crests**. Crested penguins have red eyes.

▲ *A rockhopper penguin*

Where to Visit Penguins

▲ *People can visit penguins in many zoos and aquariums.*

Penguins live south of the equator. People who live in other parts of the world see penguins only in zoos and aquariums.

For example, the Central Park Zoo in New York City has a penguin display for visitors. The penguins live in a large tank in a big house. They swim in the tank and hop up on the nearby rocks. Visitors can walk along the side of the tank. People can also watch the penguins being fed.

▲ *A penguin display in Coney Island, New York.*

Penguins in Danger

Most penguins live to be fifteen to twenty years old. Some live to be much older. Others die while they are very young.

Penguin chicks can starve if their parents do not watch them and take care of them. Young chicks are sometimes eaten by birds that live near their nests.

▲ *A baby penguin needs to be protected by a parent.*

Other animals also attack adult penguins. Seals, sea lions, sharks, and whales kill penguins for food. Some other birds and small land animals also hunt penguins.

Some types of penguins are in danger today. Each year, there are fewer and fewer of these birds. Soon there may be no more penguins left in the wild. The Humboldt, African, and Galápagos penguins are all in danger of dying out.

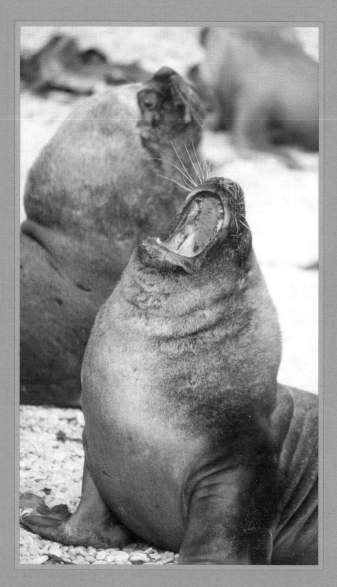

▲ *Sea lions eat penguins.*

▲ *A Galápagos penguin*

▼ *A Humboldt penguin*

41

Penguins and People

▲ Today, many people help protect penguins and the places where they live.

Long ago, many people hunted penguins. They made slippers, purses, and hats out of penguin skins. They used the birds' feathers to decorate women's clothing.

Very few people hunt penguins today, of course. But people still hurt the birds and their homes. Penguin colonies are often replaced by new roads. Some penguins die after eating garbage that people throw in the ocean.

Pollution is also harmful to penguins. Oil spills in the ocean are a great danger. The oil ruins the feathers that keep the bird warm. Many penguins die from swallowing the oil too.

People can help penguins by protecting their colonies. We can also help penguins by keeping the oceans clean.

Glossary

chicks—baby penguins

colonies—large groups of penguins that live together

crests—the yellow feathers on a crested penguin's head

equator—an imaginary line around the middle of Earth

fast—to stop eating

krill—small sea animals eaten by penguins and some whales

molting—losing and regrowing feathers each year

porpoising—leaping out of the water to breathe

tobogganing—sliding on the ice, pushing with wings and feet; a toboggan is a type of sled

Did You Know?

- When it is time to breed, penguins always return to the area where they were born.

- Most penguin eggs are white or green.

- Penguins don't have teeth.

- Because penguins have few enemies on land, they have little natural fear of humans.

The pink areas show where penguins live.

Range: Penguins live in the Southern Hemisphere—the region south of the equator—including Antarctica, New Zealand, Australia, Africa, and South America.

Species: There are seventeen kinds of penguins.

Size: The smallest penguin is the little blue penguin, or fairy penguin. It is only 12 inches (30 centimeters) tall. The largest penguin is the emperor penguin. It grows as tall as 4 feet (1.2 meters).

Diet: Penguins eat squid, fish, and krill.

Young: Most penguin mothers lay one or two eggs in nests. The emperor penguin lays only one egg.

Want to Know More?

At the Library
Crewe, Sabrina. *The Penguin.* Austin, Tex.: Raintree Steck-Vaughn, 1997.

Fowler, Allan. *These Birds Can't Fly.* Danbury, Conn.: Children's Press, 1998.

McMillan, Bruce. *Penguins at Home: Gentoos of Antarctica.* New York: Houghton Mifflin, 1993.

Walker-Hodge, Judith. *Penguins.* New York: Barrons Juveniles, 1999.

On the Web
Penguins
http://www.seaworld.org/Penguins/pageone.html
For information about the behavior and eating habits of penguins

Virtual Antarctica Science: Penguins
http://www.terraquest.com/va/science/penguins/penguins.html
For information about penguins and photographs of penguins

Through the Mail
Falkland Islands Environmental Research Unit
P.O. Box 434
Stanley, Falkland Islands
To get information about penguins and other wildlife on the Falkland Islands

On the Road
Oregon Zoo
4001 S.W. Canyon Road
Portland, OR 97221
503/226-1561
To visit the Penguinarium and more than thirty-five Humboldt penguins, the most endangered penguin species

Index

About the Author

Lucia Raatma received her bachelor's degree in English literature from the University of South Carolina and her master's degree in cinema studies from New York University.

She has written a wide range of books for young people. When she is not researching or writing, she enjoys going to movies, playing tennis, and spending time with her husband, daughter, and golden retriever.

CARMEL CLAY PUBLIC LIBRARY
55 4th Avenue SE
Carmel, IN 46032
(317) 844-3361
Renewal Line: (317) 814-3936
www.carmel.lib.in.us